YOUR PASSPORT TO

EL SALVADOR

by Sarah Cords

CONTENT CONSULTANT

Cecilia Menjívar, PhD
Professor
Dorothy L. Meier Social Equities Chair
University of California, Los Angeles

CAPSTONE PRESS
a capstone imprint

Capstone Captivate is published by Capstone Press, an imprint of Capstone.
1710 Roe Crest Drive
North Mankato, Minnesota 56003
www.capstonepub.com

Library of Congress Cataloging-in-Publication Data
Names: Cords, Sarah Statz, 1974- author.
Title: Your passport to El Salvador / Sarah Cords.
Description: North Mankato, Minnesota : Capstone Press, [2021] | Series:
    World passport | Audience: Grades 4-6
Identifiers: LCCN 2020001008 (print) | LCCN 2020001009 (ebook) | ISBN
    9781496684035 ; (hardcover) | ISBN 9781496687951 ; (paperback) | ISBN
    9781496684547 ; (pdf)
Subjects: LCSH: El Salvador--Description and travel--Juvenile literature. |
    El Salvador--Social life and customs--Juvenile literature.
Classification: LCC F1484.3 .C67 2021 (print) | LCC F1484.3 (ebook) | DDC
    972.84--dc23
LC record available at https://lccn.loc.gov/2020001008
LC ebook record available at https://lccn.loc.gov/2020001009

Image Credits
AP Images: Richard Drew, 13; iStockphoto: lanabyko, cover (bottom); Newscom: Album/Oronoz, 10; Red Line Editorial: 5; Shutterstock Images: carlos.araujo, 27, Daniel Andis, 9, Danita Delmont, 12, De Jongh Photography, 11, Filip Bjorkman, cover (map), Guayo Fuentes, 17, 28, HMedia, 7, Joey Villaflor, 6, Kobby Dagan, 18, Millenius, 25, Milosz Maslanka, 15, 21, StudioGShock, 22, Thiago B Trevisan, 19, Wee design, cover (flag)
Design Elements: iStockphoto, Shutterstock Images

Editorial Credits
Editor: Jamie Hudalla; Designer: Colleen McLaren

Printed in the United States of America.
PA117

CONTENTS

Words in **bold** are in the glossary.

CHAPTER ONE

WELCOME TO EL SALVADOR!

A tall volcano towers over San Salvador. Beautiful churches and buildings line the streets. The city has many art museums. San Salvador is high in the mountains. It is the capital of El Salvador.

El Salvador is located in Central America. The country is nestled between Honduras and Guatemala. It could fit inside the United States 467 times. More than 6 million people live there. Its climate is **tropical**. The temperature is mostly hot. The rainy season is from May to October. During this time, rain falls nearly every day.

MAP OF EL SALVADOR

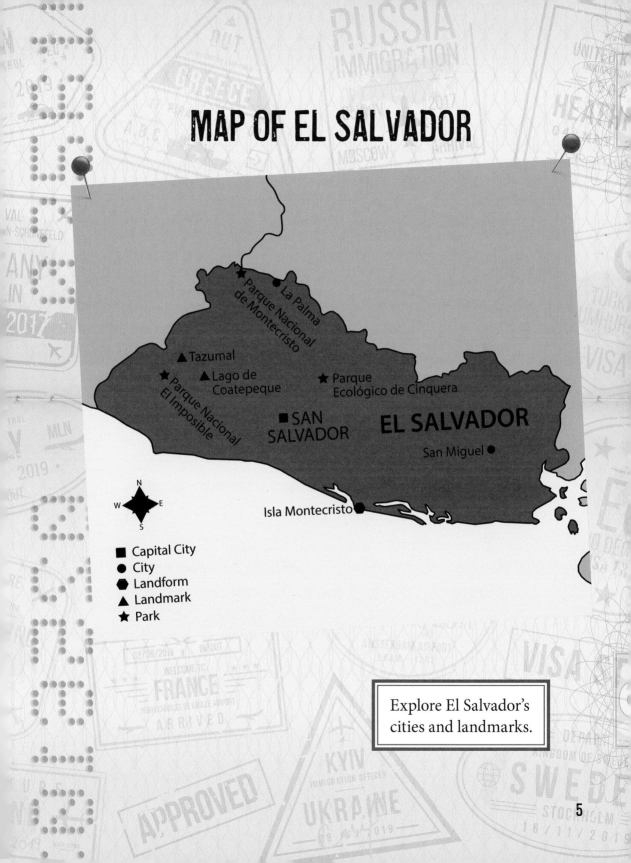

La Palma

Parque Nacional de Montecristo ★

▲ Tazumal

Parque Nacional El Imposible ★

Lago de Coatepeque ▲

Parque Ecológico de Cinquera ★

■ SAN SALVADOR

EL SALVADOR

San Miguel ●

N
W E
S

Isla Montecristo ●

■ Capital City
● City
⬢ Landform
▲ Landmark
★ Park

Explore El Salvador's cities and landmarks.

San Salvador has beautiful, old buildings.

Most of the people who live in El Salvador are *mestizo*. They have both European and **indigenous ancestors**. Some people speak native languages such as Nawat and Nahuatl. Others speak Spanish. Spanish is the country's official language.

Visitors can find beautiful natural areas in El Salvador. The country has parks with rare flowers and birds. People love to hike in the mountains. They can also surf in the Pacific Ocean.

FACT

More than 400 species of birds live in El Salvador.

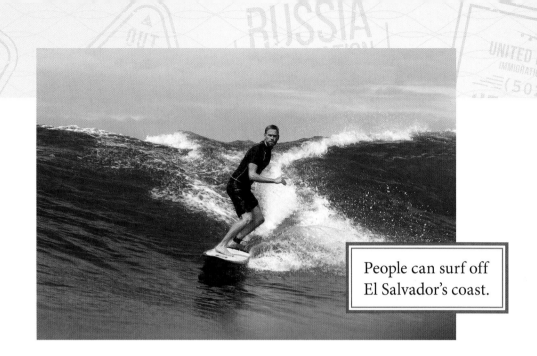

People can surf off El Salvador's coast.

FACT FILE

OFFICIAL NAME: REPUBLIC OF EL SALVADOR

POPULATION: 6,187,271

LAND AREA: 8,124 SQ. MI. (21,040 SQ KM)

CAPITAL: SAN SALVADOR

MONEY: U.S. DOLLAR AND SALVADORAN COLÓN

GOVERNMENT: Republic, with a president as the head of the government.

LANGUAGE: SPANISH, NAWAT, AND NAHUATL

GEOGRAPHY: El Salvador is located between Honduras and Guatemala. It is mountainous, with two ranges that run side by side in the middle of the country.

NATURAL RESOURCES: El Salvador has wood, cattle, sugarcane, coffee, cotton, and corn.

CHAPTER TWO

HISTORY OF EL SALVADOR

For 10,000 years, people have lived in the region that is now El Salvador. A group of people called the Olmecs settled there as early as 2000 **BCE**. Then, people from Mexico arrived in the 1000s **CE**. They were known as the Pipils. They called the land Cuscatlán. From 1000 BCE to the 1500s CE, people of the **Maya** civilization also lived there. They built roads and cities in the area.

SPANISH RULE

In 1524, Pedro de Alvarado arrived from Spain. He started a war with the Pipils. Spain wanted the land for its gold, agricultural products, and farm land. This would make Spain wealthier. By 1528, the Spanish invaders had won the war. The Spanish named the region El Salvador.

People can visit the remains of Maya farmhouses in El Salvador.

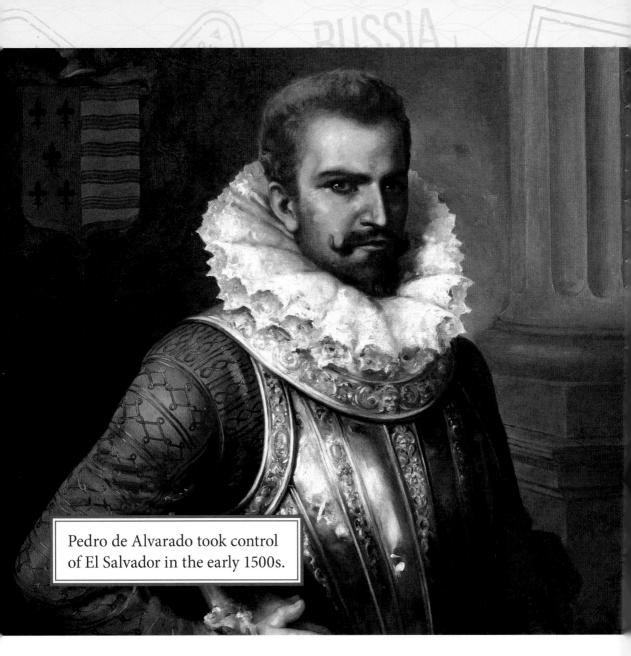

Pedro de Alvarado took control
of El Salvador in the early 1500s.

In 1808, the emperor of France invaded Spain. The
war in Spain weakened the control of the Spanish
throughout Central America. In 1821, the people of
El Salvador declared their **independence**.

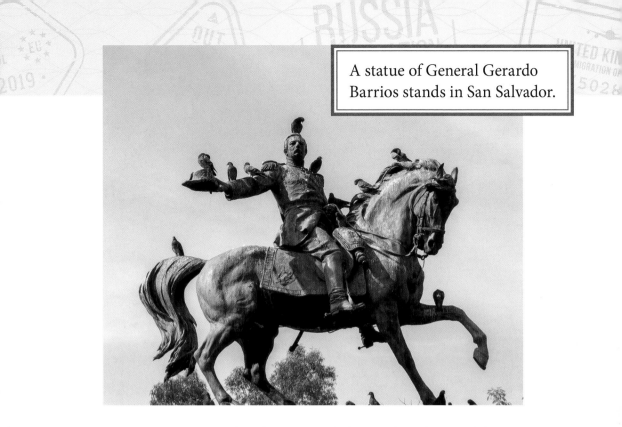

A statue of General Gerardo Barrios stands in San Salvador.

In 1824, El Salvador joined the Federal Republic of Central America. Guatemala, Nicaragua, Costa Rica, and Honduras belonged to this group. The leaders of this republic could not agree on how to rule. In 1841, El Salvador left this group. It became a **sovereign** nation.

COFFEE BEANS AND CIVIL WARS

In 1858, General Gerardo Barrios became El Salvador's president. He decided growing and selling coffee to other countries would make more money for the country.

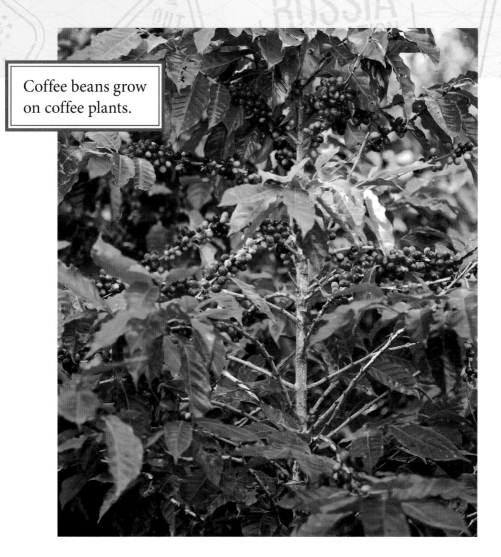

Coffee beans grow on coffee plants.

By the 1920s, coffee was the country's main crop. Coffee made up 90 percent of El Salvador's **exports** to other countries.

Nayib Bukele became El Salvador's president in 2019.

In the 1980s, a civil war broke out. At that time, the military and government had too much control. People with little money or power fought for more rights. The war lasted 12 years. Many people fled the country. They came to the United States. When the war ended, people tried to live together peacefully. In 2019, Nayib Bukele became president. Presidents can stay in office for five years in El Salvador.

CHAPTER THREE

EXPLORE EL SALVADOR

El Salvador has ancient landmarks, vibrant towns, and natural areas. The Maya built an ancient settlement called Tazumal. It has several pyramids. Other remains of the city have been discovered. These include ball courts and statues.

La Palma is a town in the Sierra Madre mountain range. The town is known for its art and **murals**. There are many hiking trails with pine trees around it. Other towns lie along the coast. Costa del Sol and El Tunco are coastal towns. They have popular beaches.

Tourists can visit the impressive Maya structures at Tazumal.

PARKS AND RESERVES

PARQUE NACIONAL DE MONTECRISTO: Located in the mountainous region of the country. Some animals that don't live anywhere else in the country live in this park.

ISLA MONTECRISTO: A tiny island in the Pacific, just off the coast. It is a wonderful place to watch birds.

PARQUE NACIONAL EL IMPOSIBLE: A forest park that contains more than 400 types of trees and 100 types of mammals.

PARQUE ECOLÓGICO DE CINQUERA: A park with nearly 10,000 acres (4,000 hectares), roughly the size of 7,500 football fields! It is located near Cinquera, a historical village.

MOUNTAINS AND VOLCANOES

Mountains cover El Salvador. The country is sometimes called the Land of Volcanoes. It has more than 20 active volcanoes. One of the most beautiful lakes in El Salvador is Lago de Coatepeque. Coatepeque is a volcano. Thousands of years ago, the volcano erupted. A crater formed in its side. Over time, the crater filled with water. It became a lake.

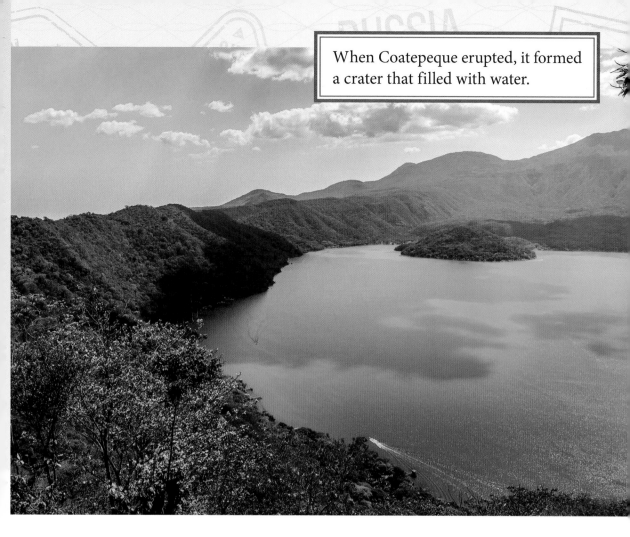

When Coatepeque erupted, it formed a crater that filled with water.

VOLCANOES

The volcanoes in El Salvador are part of the Pacific Ring of Fire. One of the most famous parks in the country features several volcanoes. This is the Cerro Verde National Park. While there, visitors can hike up two volcanoes, Izalco and Santa Ana. Santa Ana is the tallest volcano in the country.

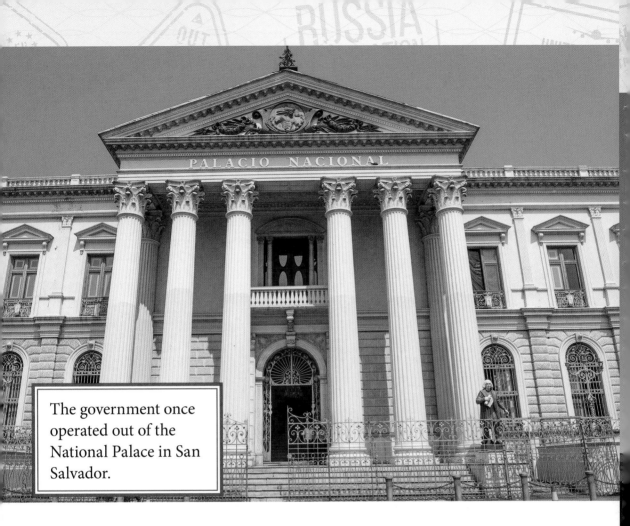

The government once operated out of the National Palace in San Salvador.

THE CAPITAL CITY

The capital of El Salvador is San Salvador. More than two million people live in and near the city. Although the city was built in 1528, not all of its buildings are old. Because of earthquakes, many parts of the city have been rebuilt. Today, San Salvador has beautiful buildings, such as the large cathedral Catedral Metropolitana.

Catedral Metropolitana was opened to the public in 1999.

CHAPTER FOUR

DAILY LIFE

Many people in El Salvador live outside the cities. Farms scatter the plains of the country. A lot of farmers grow coffee. Some of these farmers work together. They form coffee cooperatives. These cooperatives help them earn more money for their coffee.

MINING

Gold and copper mining used to be part of El Salvador's **economy**. But in 2017, a law was passed that banned mining. Many people worked together to pass this law. Citizens and government leaders thought the ban was a good idea. Mining can cause damage to the environment. The people of El Salvador hoped this ban would protect their environment.

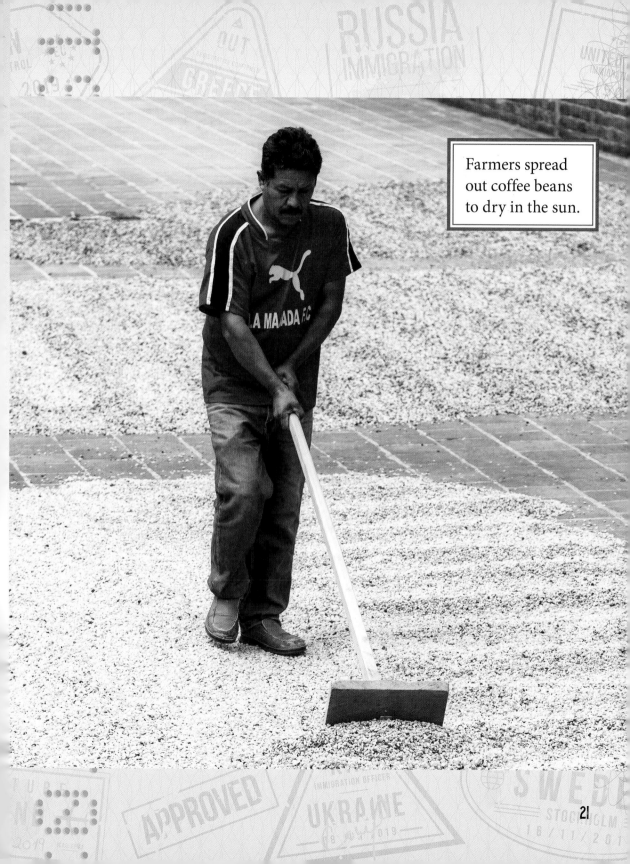

Farmers spread out coffee beans to dry in the sun.

Many people put pork and cheese in pupusas.

TRADITIONAL CLOTHES AND FOOD

People often wear light clothing. The lightweight fabric helps the wearer stay cool in the country's hot weather. Traditional clothing often has embroidery, or decorations made with needles and thread. These outfits are usually colorful and are worn when performing traditional dances.

FACT

One of El Salvador's exports is indigo. This blue dye comes from the anil plant.

A popular food is *pupusa*. Corn tortillas make up the outside of pupusas. People fill the tortillas with beans, pork, and cheese.

THE SCHOOL SYSTEM

Kids in El Salvador usually start school around age 7. Some kids can attend up to nine years of school. Then they can leave or go on to get their high school education. They may then attend college. Many go to the Universidad de El Salvador. It was founded in 1841. It is one of the best colleges in the country.

FRESCO DE ENSALADA DE FRUTAS

Fresco de ensalada de frutas is a traditional fruit salad drink. Ask an adult for help preparing the fruit for this recipe.

Ensalada Ingredients:

- One 20-ounce can of crushed pineapple
- 2 apples cut into small pieces
- 2 oranges peeled and cut into small pieces
- ¼ cup orange juice
- A splash of lemon juice
- 1 cup of cantaloupe cut into small pieces
- ¼ cup sugar
- 8 cups of water
- A pinch of salt

Ensalada Directions:

1. Combine pineapples, apples, oranges, and cantaloupe in large bowl.
2. Add orange juice, lemon juice, sugar, water, and pinch of salt.
3. Stir and then refrigerate for one hour.

CHAPTER FIVE

HOLIDAYS AND CELEBRATIONS

September 15 is Día de la Independencia. The people of El Salvador celebrate their independence from Spain. People march in parades. At night, they shoot off colorful fireworks.

A popular indigenous celebration is the Día de la Cruz. This holiday is celebrated at the beginning of the rainy season, on May 3. People decorate crosses with flowers and make offerings of fruit. They honor the earth and celebrate the harvest.

RELIGIOUS HOLIDAYS

In El Salvador, 80 percent of people are Christians. About half the people who live there are Roman Catholics. Even if people do not belong to a religion, some still celebrate religious holidays.

On Día de la Independencia, people wave El Salvador's flag during military marches.

Many Catholics honor saints. In the Catholic religion, saints are people who are considered very holy. In the city of San Miguel, people celebrate the Queen of the Peace Day. It takes place the last Saturday in November. It is a day to honor Mary, the mother of Jesus. Mary is very important to Catholics.

CHAPTER SIX

SPORTS AND RECREATION

Soccer is the most popular sport in El Salvador. There are 10 teams in the country's top league. One soccer stadium in San Salvador can hold 45,000 fans! That is even more than Fenway Park in Boston, where the Red Sox play baseball.

Adventure sports are also popular in El Salvador. People enjoy hiking in the mountains. For those who live near the ocean, people often swim and surf in the Pacific Ocean's big waves. Many people also go kayaking on the beautiful lakes.

TYPES OF MUSIC

Salvadorans listen to a variety of music. Many people know songs passed down by their ancestors.

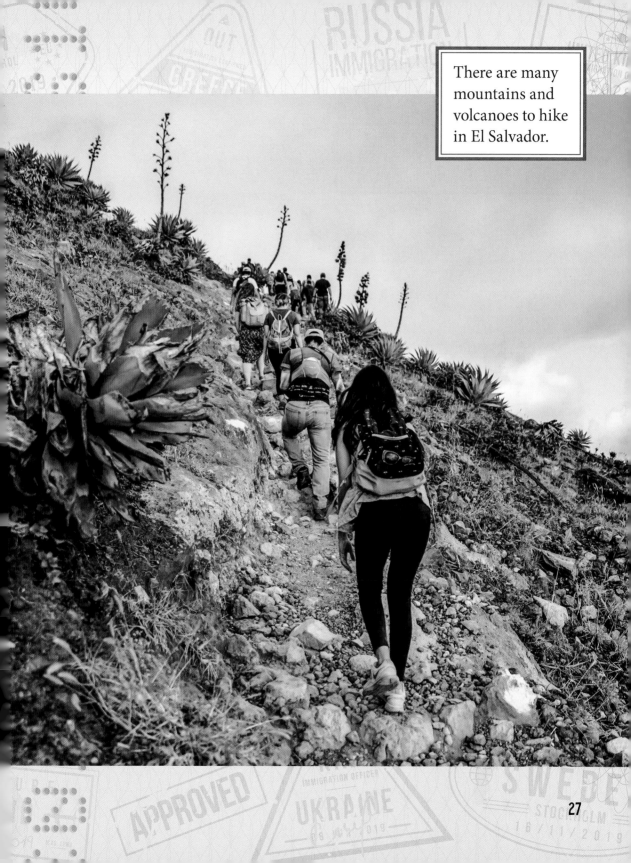

There are many mountains and volcanoes to hike in El Salvador.

Musicians perform at Puerta de la Libertad in El Salvador.

One type of music is called cumbia of El Salvador. This music mixes African, Spanish, and indigenous styles. Some people also enjoy Salvadoran hip-hop.

From its vibrant towns to its tall volcanoes, there is a lot to see in El Salvador. With its delicious food and beautiful views, El Salvador is a wonderful place to visit and live.

TRIPA CHUCA

Tripa Chuca is a game played by children in El Salvador. To play, you need two people, paper, and two different colored markers.

1. All over the paper, in random order, write numbers one through 20 in one marker color.
2. On the same sheet of paper, repeat step one with the other marker color.
3. The first player circles number one and then draws a line to the number one in the other color and circles it.
4. The second player uses the other color marker and circles number two. The second player draws a line to the other number two and circles it. But the line that player draws cannot touch or cross the line the first player drew.
5. The players take turns circling and connecting the numbers in sequence. Eventually things get very messy!
6. The player who touches another number or line first loses.

GLOSSARY

**ancestors
(AN-sess-turs)**
the relatives that people
came from

BCE/CE
BCE means Before
Common Era, or before
year one. CE means
Common Era, or after
year one

**economy
(i-KAH-nuh-mee)**
wealth and resources in
a country

exports (EK-sports)
products a country sells
and ships to other countries

**independence
(in-di-PEN-duhnss)**
the freedom a country has
to govern itself

**indigenous
(in-DIJ-uh-nuhs)**
first people, plants, and
animals to live in a country

Maya (MY-yah)
a nation of people in
Mexico and Central
America that lasted from
7000 BCE to 1524 CE

murals (MYU-ruhls)
large paintings usually on a
wall or large surface

sovereign (SOV-ruhn)
independent and
governs itself

**tropical
(TRAH-pi-kuhl)**
a climate that is very hot
and humid

READ MORE

Mattern, Joanne. *El Salvador*. Minneapolis, MN: Jump, Inc.! 2019.

Nargi, Lela. *Volcanoes*. Washington DC: National Geographic, 2018.

Yasuda, Anita. *Ancient Civilizations: Aztecs, Maya, Incas!* White River Junction, VT: Nomad Press, 2019.

INTERNET SITES

BrainPop!: Maya Civilization
https://www.brainpop.com/socialstudies/worldhistory/mayacivilization

DK Find Out!: Volcanoes
https://www.dkfindout.com/us/earth/volcanoes/where-are-earths-volcanoes

National Geographic Kids: El Salvador
https://kids.nationalgeographic.com/explore/countries/el-salvador

INDEX

OTHER BOOKS IN THIS SERIES

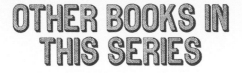

YOUR PASSPORT TO CHINA
YOUR PASSPORT TO ECUADOR
YOUR PASSPORT TO ETHIOPIA
YOUR PASSPORT TO FRANCE
YOUR PASSPORT TO IRAN
YOUR PASSPORT TO KENYA
YOUR PASSPORT TO PERU
YOUR PASSPORT TO RUSSIA
YOUR PASSPORT TO SPAIN